About
Skill Builders
Algebra II

by Brenda Gardner

Welcome to RBP Books' Skill Builders series. Like our Summer Bridge Activities collection, the Skill Builders series is designed to make learning both fun and rewarding.

Skill Builders Algebra II provides students with focused practice to help them reinforce and develop math skills. Each Skill Builders volume is grade-level appropriate, with clear examples and instructions to guide the lesson. In accordance with NCTM standards, the algebra exercises in this book cover a variety of math skills, including graphing, equations, monomials and polynomials, exponents, factoring, radicals, working with imaginary numbers, quadratic equations, exponential and logarithmic functions, and conics.

A critical thinking section includes problem-solving exercises to help develop higher-order thinking skills.

Learning is more effective when approached with an element of fun and enthusiasm—just as most children approach life. That's why the Skill Builders combine entertaining and academically sound exercises and fun themes to make reviewing basic skills fun and effective, for both you and your budding scholars.

Table of Contents

Graphing Linear Equations Using Tables

Example:

Graph 2x = 4 – 2y using three points.

1. Solve for y.

   2x = 4 – 2y
   2x + 2y = 4
   2y = 4 – 2x
   y = 2 – x

x	y = 2 – x	y
2	y = 2 – 2	0
-2	y = 2 – (-2)	4
0	y = 2 – 0	2

   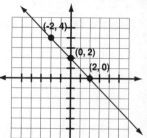

2. Pick any three numbers for x. (We'll pick 2, -2, 0.)
   Replace x with the chosen numbers. Find values for y.

3. You now have three points: (2,0), (-2,4), (0,2).
   Plot those three points. Draw your line.

Graph the following linear equations using three points.

1. y – x = 2

x	y =	y

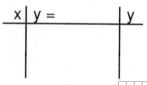

2. 2x – y = 0

x	y =	y

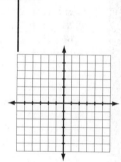

3. 6x + 2y = 10

x	y =	y

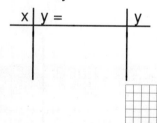

4. 3y – 12 = -9x

x	y =	y

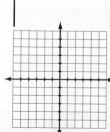

Graphing Linear Equations Using Intercepts

Example:

Graph 3x + 4y = 12 using x- and y-intercepts.

1. To find the x-intercept, replace y with 0. Find the value for x.
   3x + 4(0) = 12   3x = 12   x = 4 (4,0)

2. To find the y-intercept, replace x with 0. Find the value for y.
   3(0) + 4y = 12   4y = 12   y = 3 (0,3)

3. Plot the intercepts. Draw your line.

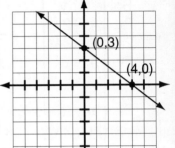

Graph using x- and y-intercepts.

1. 2y − x = 2   **2.** 2x − 5y = 10   **3.** 3y = 5x − 15

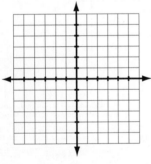   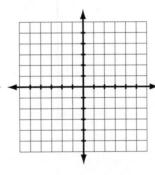   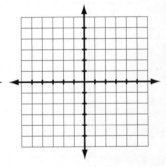

4. -1y − 3x = 3   **5.** 4x − 2y = 16   **6.** -3y + 18 = -9x

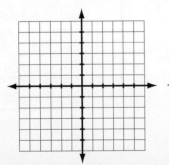   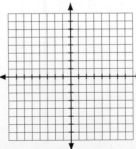   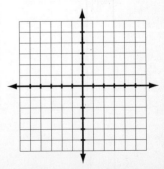

Slope

Slope is equal to $\dfrac{\text{change in y}}{\text{change in x}}$

Find the slope of the line containing (8,-2), (-4,4).

$$\frac{\text{Change in y}}{\text{Change in x}} = \frac{-2 - 4}{8 - (-4)} = \frac{-6}{12} = \frac{-1}{2} \text{ (Reduce if possible.)}$$

Find the slope.

1. (5,2), (-3,6)   **2.** (-1,3), (2,4)

3. (-4,-6), (2,0)   **4.** (-1,-3), (5,-3)

5. (2,6), (4,8)   **6.** (3,5), (-2,-1)

7. (8,6), (12,-2)   **8.** (-4,-5), (0,2)

3

The slope-intercept form is $y = mx + b$
where m = slope and b = y-intercept.

Graph $2x - 3y = 6$ using y-intercept and slope.

1. Solve for y. $y = \frac{2}{3}x - 2$

2. $m = \frac{2}{3}$ $b = -2$

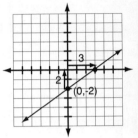

3. Start at b on y-axis. Use slope to find second point.

Graph using y-intercept and slope.

1. $y = 2x - 5$

2. $y = -\frac{2}{3}x + 1 =$

3. $y = -\frac{4}{5}x$

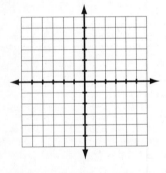
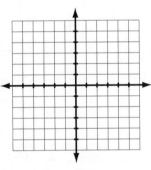
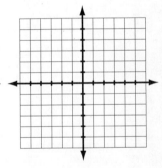

4. $2x + 5y = 10$

5. $-3x + 3y = 9$

6. $x - 4y = 8$

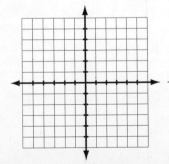
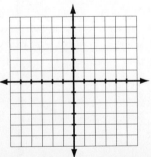
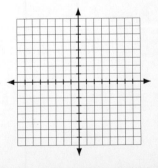

4

Solving Linear Systems by Graphing

Example:

Solve $y = x - 5$ by graphing.
         $2x + y = 4$

Graph using slope and intercept
or x- and y-intercepts.

The solution is where they cross. **(3,-2)**

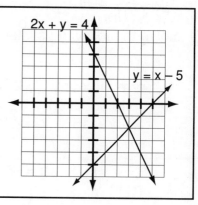

Solve by graphing.

1. $x + 2y = 4$
          $2x + y = -1$

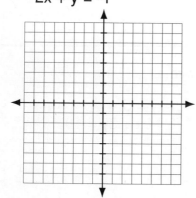

2. $x + y = 1$
          $-2x = y$

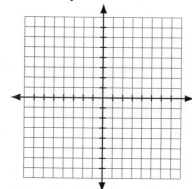

3. $3x - 2y = 6$
          $y = 3$

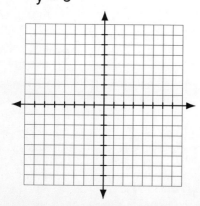

4. $y = \frac{1}{2}x - 2$
          $x - 2y = 8$

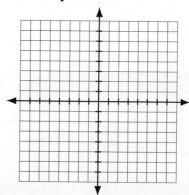

5

Solving Linear Systems
by Substitution

Example:

Solve the following system: $2x - 5y = 9$
                                $x - y = 15$

1. Solve for x or y
   in one equation.
   If $x - y = 15$,
   then $x = 15 + y$

2. Substitute into other
   equation. Solve.
   $2x - 5y = 9$
   $2(15 + y) - 5y = 9$
   $30 + 2y - 5y = 9$
   $30 - 3y = 9$
   $-3y = -21$
   $y = 7$

3. Plug into either
   equation.
   $x = 15 + y$
   $x = 15 + 7$
   $x = 22$

4. Check solution. **(22,7)** $2(22) - 5(7) \stackrel{?}{=} 9$ $22 - 7 \stackrel{?}{=} 15$
                                       $44 - 35 \stackrel{?}{=} 9$ $15 = 15 ✓$
                                               $9 = 9 ✓$

Solve by substitution. Check your answers.

1. $x = 3 + 2y$
         $2x + 4y = 14$

2. $y = 5 - x$
         $-2x + 3y = 10$

3. $-3x + 5y = 2$
         $y - 2x = 6$

4. $3x = 4 - y$
         $-5x + 8y = -26$

Solving Linear Systems by Elimination

Solve the following system: -2x + 5y = 11 (equation 1)
                                 4x – 2y = 10 (equation 2)

1. Eliminate a set of   **2.** Add (3) to (2).   **3.** Plug into either
variables.   -4x + 10y = 22 (3)   equation.
2[-2x + 5y = 11] (1)   + 4x – 2y = 10 (2)   -2x + 5(4) = 11 (1)
-4x + 10y = 22 (3)   ──────────────   -2x + 20 = 11
                                   8y = 32   -2x = -9
                                   y = 4 $x = \dfrac{9}{2}$

4. Check solution. ($\dfrac{9}{2}$,4)

$-2(\dfrac{9}{2}) + 5(4) \overset{?}{=} 11$ $4(\dfrac{9}{2}) - 2(4) \overset{?}{=} 10$
$\qquad -9 + 20 \overset{?}{=} 11$ $\qquad 18 - 8 \overset{?}{=} 10$
$\qquad\qquad 11 = 11 \checkmark$ $\qquad\qquad 10 = 10 \checkmark$

Solve by elimination. Check your answers.

1.   2x – 3y = -9   **2.**   2x – y = 7
         4x + 9y = -13   4x + 5y = 7

3.   2x + 4y = 14   **4.**   4x – 3y = 16
         4x + y = 14   5x + 17y = 20

Algebra II Grades 6–8—RBP0830

Adding and Subtracting Polynomials

Example:

Add
$(-6x^3 + 4x^2 - 2x + 7) + (7x^2 - x - 4)$
$= -6x^3 + 4x^2 - 2x + 7 + 7x^2 - x - 4$
$= \mathbf{-6x^3 + 11x^2 - 3x + 3}$

Subtract
$(8y^2 + 4y^3 + 2y) - (-4y^2 + 3y^4 - 8y)$
$= 8y^2 + 4y^3 + 2y + 4y^2 - 3y^4 + 8y$
$= \mathbf{-3y^4 + 4y^3 + 12y^2 + 10y}$

Add or subtract.

1. $(4a^5 - 2a^3) + (2a^3 - 7a + 3)$

2. $(-4x^5 - 13x^2 - 14) + (5x^6 + 5x^3 + 7x^2)$

3. $(-11x^2 + 19x + 18) + (-8x^2 - 14x - 11)$

4. $(13x^5 + 12x^4 - 12x^3) + (12x^6 + 20x^4 + 16x)$

5. $(-15x^2 - 5x + 10) + (16x^2 + 4x - 11) + (-19x^2 + 19x - 20)$

6. $(17x^2 + 18x + 4) - (10x^2 + 15x + 6)$

7. $(15x^2 + 11x + 10) - (-14x^2 + 7x - 4)$

8. $(-13x^6 + 18x^5 + 7x^4 + 14x^2 - 8x) - (-14x^7 + 19x^2 - 11)$

9. $(4x^2 + 5x + 8) - (12x^2 + 19x + 13)$

10. Subtract $-20x^4 - 6x^3 + 17$ from $15x^7 + 12x^5 - 8x + 3$.

Properties of Exponents

$$(a^x)^y = a^{xy} \qquad\qquad a^x \cdot a^y = a^{x+y} \qquad\qquad \frac{a^x}{a^y} = a^{x-y}$$

$$(ab)^x = a^x b^x \qquad\qquad (\frac{a}{b})^x = \frac{a^x}{b^x}$$

$$a^{-x} = \frac{1}{a^x} \qquad\qquad \frac{1}{a^{-x}} = a^x$$

$$(\frac{2x}{3})^{-3} = \frac{2^{-3}x^{-3}}{3^{-3}} = \frac{3^3}{2^3 x^3} = \frac{27}{8x^3}$$

Simplify. Write answers with positive exponents.

1. $(x^2)^3$

2. $(\frac{x}{y})^4$

3. $a^3 \cdot a^5$

4. w^{-5}

5. $(2b)^4$

6. $\frac{b^3}{b^5}$

7. $(3d^5)^2$

8. $(\frac{2}{x})^{-1}$

9. $\frac{1}{m^{-14}}$

10. $k^3 \cdot \frac{k^4}{k^5}$

9

Multiplying and Dividing Monomials

Multiply $\quad$ $-3x^2(-6x^2 + 2x - 11)$

$\quad\quad\quad\quad = (-3)(-6)x^{2+2} + (-3)(2)x^{2+1} + (-3)(-11)x^2$

$\quad\quad\quad\quad = \mathbf{18x^4 - 6x^3 + 33x^2}$

Divide $\quad$ $\dfrac{10x^{11} - 25x^5 + 15x}{10x^2} = \dfrac{10x^{11-2}}{10} - \dfrac{25x^{5-2}}{10} + \dfrac{15x^{1-2}}{10} =$

$\quad\quad\quad\quad x^9 - \dfrac{5x^3}{2} + \dfrac{3x^{-1}}{2}$

Multiply or divide.

1. $\quad (-6x)(10x + 6)$

2. $\quad 4x^2(10x^3 - 12x^2 - x + 8)$

3. $\quad (-5x - 4)(-3x)$

4. $\quad -9x^3(-6x^2 + 10)$

5. $\quad -x(9x^2 + 3x - 5)$

6. $\quad (4x^{10} + 6x^6 + 8x^3) \div 4x^3$

7. $\quad (-30x^{12} - 35x^9 + 45x^2) \div 10x^2$

8. $\quad (8x^{10} - 8x^7 - 48x^4) \div 16x$

9. $\quad (-18x^{12} + 27x^{11} - 6x^5 + 21x^3) \div 9x^3$

10. $\quad (33x^6 - 44x^5 + 44x^4 + 99x^3 + 34x^2) \div 11x^3$

Example:

$(-7x^2 + 3x - 7)(-8x + 10)$

$= (-7x^2)(-8x) + (-7x^2)(10) + (3x)(-8x) + (3x)(10) + (-7)(-8x) + (-7)(10)$

$= 56x^3 - 70x^2 - 24x^2 + 30x + 56x - 70$

$= \mathbf{56x^3 - 94x^2 + 86x - 70}$

Multiply.

1. $(2x + 7)(8x - 7)$

2. $(-10x^4 - 7x^2)(4x - 4)$

3. $(-4x^2 - 3x - 11)(12x - 2)$

4. $(10x^4 - 12x^3 + 4)(4x^2 - 4x + 2)$

5. $(-12)(2x - 6)$

6. $(4x^4 + 7x^3)(-11x + 4)$

7. $(11x^2 - 7x + 8)(4x + 7)$

8. $(-10x^2 + 12x + 9)(-10x^2 - 5x - 10)$

Example:

$$(2x^3 + 7x^2 - x - 4) \div (2x + 1)$$

1.
$$\begin{array}{r} 1x^2 \\ 2x + 1 \overline{)\, 2x^3 + 7x^2 - x - 4} \\ \underline{-(2x^3 + 1x^2)} \\ 6x^2 - x \end{array}$$

2.
$$\begin{array}{r} 1x^2 + 3x \\ 2x + 1 \overline{)\, 2x^3 + 7x^2 - x - 4} \\ \underline{-(2x^3 + 1x^2)} \\ 6x^2 - x \\ \underline{-(6x^2 + 3x)} \\ -4x - 4 \end{array}$$

3.
$$\begin{array}{r} 1x^2 + 3x - 2 - \dfrac{2}{2x+1} \\ 2x + 1 \overline{)\, 2x^3 + 7x^2 - x - 4} \\ \underline{-(2x^3 + 1x^2)} \\ 6x^2 - x \\ \underline{-(6x^2 + 3x)} \\ -4x - 4 \\ \underline{-(-4x - 2)} \\ -2 \end{array}$$

Divide.

1. $(-3x^3 - 15x^2 + 108x) \div (x - 4)$

2. $(-x^3 - 8x^2 - 16x) \div (x + 4)$

3. $(4x^3 + 7x^2 - 14x + 6) \div (4x - 1)$

4. $(-2x^3 - 42x^2 - 216x) \div (x + 12)$

5. $(-3x^3 + 3x^2 + 18x + 5) \div (x - 3)$

Example:

$$9x^3y^5 - 15x^2y^3 - 12xy^4 = \mathbf{3xy^3(3x^2y^2 - 5x - 4y)}$$

Check: $3xy^3(3x^2y^2) + 3xy^3(-5x) + 3xy^3(-4y) = 9x^3y^5 - 15x^2y^3 - 12xy^4$

Factor. Check your answer.

1. $3a^2 + 3a - 6$

2. $2y^4 + 14y^3$

3. $4b^3 - 8b^2 + 16b$

4. $30e^2 - 12ef + 6e^2f^2$

5. $4d^3 - 4ad + 4a^2$

6. $28w^3x + 8w^4x$

7. $12r^6 + 8r^7 - 32r^8 + 36r^9$

8. $10cde + 20cef - 30ceg$

Example:

$$6x^2 - x - 12$$
$$= (2x - 3)(3x + 4)$$

Check: $(2x)(3x) + (2x)(4) + (-3)(3x) + (-3)(4)$
$$= 6x^2 + 8x - 9x - 12$$
$$= 6x^2 - x - 12$$

Factor. Check your answer.

1. $x^2 - 2x - 63$

2. $x^2 - 10x + 25$

3. $x^2 + 2x + 1$

4. $2x^2 - 5x - 3$

5. $8x^2 - 6x - 9$

6. $3x^2 + 10x - 8$

7. $12x^2 + 23x + 10$

8. $6x^2 + 23x + 20$

Factoring Trinomials

$$3x^3 + 15x^2 + 18x$$
$$= 3x(x^2 + 5x + 6)$$
$$= \mathbf{3x(x + 2)(x + 3)}$$

Factor.

1. $x^3 - 5x^2 - 36x$

2. $3x^2 - 24x - 144$

3. $-4x^3 + 64x^2 - 256x$

4. $3x^3 - 6x^2 - 144x$

5. $x^3 - 3x^2 - 88x$

6. $-3x^3 + 45x^2 - 150x$

7. $6x^4 - 54x^3 - 60x^2$

8. $2x^5 - 46x^4 + 264x^3$

Factoring Binomials

Difference of Squares

$A^2 - B^2$

$= (A+B)(A-B)$

$4x^2 - 9y^4$

$= (2x+3y^2)(2x-3y^2)$

Difference of Cubes

$A^3 - B^3$

$= (A-B)(A^2+AB+B^2)$

$x^3 - 8b^6$

$= (x-2b^2)(x^2+2ab+4b^4)$

Sum of Cubes

$A^3 + B^3$

$= (A+B)(A^2-AB+B^2)$

$c^9 + d^6$

$= (c^3+d^2)(c^6-c^3d^2+d^4)$

Factor.

1. $x^2 - 121$

2. $4x^2 - 81$

3. $81y^4 - 64x^2y^2$

4. $a^3 + 27$

5. $b^3c^6 - 1$

6. $27z^3 + 1$

7. $125c^6 - 8d^9$

8. $64 - 125x^3$

9. $\dfrac{1}{36} - m^2$

10. $2y^4 - 128y$

Multiplying Rational Expressions

Example:

$$\frac{3xy^2}{4z} \cdot \frac{2z^3}{9x^2} = \frac{6xy^2z^3}{36x^2z} = \frac{y^2z^2}{6x}$$

$$\frac{x^2 + 8x + 15}{8x^2 - 10x + 3} \cdot \frac{4x - 3}{x + 7} = \frac{(x + 3)(x + 5)(4x - 3)}{(2x - 1)(4x - 3)(x + 7)} = \frac{(x + 3)(x + 5)}{(2x - 1)(x + 7)}$$

Reduce your answer to lowest terms.

1. $\dfrac{6x}{y^3z^2} \cdot \dfrac{7y}{3x^3}$

2. $\dfrac{8m^5n}{5p^2} \cdot \dfrac{15mp}{24m^2n^4}$

3. $\dfrac{48f^5}{84f^3} \cdot \dfrac{18f^6}{48f^3}$

4. $\dfrac{w + 3}{w^2 - 4} \cdot \dfrac{w + 2}{w^2 - 9}$

5. $\dfrac{f^2 - 81}{f^2 + 8f - 9} \cdot \dfrac{f^2 - 13f + 40}{-7f^4 + 56f^3}$

6. $\dfrac{-8d^3 + 16d}{-4d} \cdot \dfrac{3d^2 - 3d}{15d^3 - 15d^2}$

Algebra II Grades 6–8—RBP0830

Example:

$$\frac{4c^2d}{5e^3} \div \frac{8cd^2}{15e} = \frac{4c^2d}{5e^3} \cdot \frac{15e}{8cd^2} = \frac{60c^2de}{40cd^2e^3} = \frac{3c}{2de^2}$$

$$\frac{\dfrac{5y^2}{y+7}}{\dfrac{10y}{y-2}} = \frac{5y^2}{y+7} \div \frac{10y}{y-2} = \frac{5y^2}{y+7} \cdot \frac{y-2}{10y} = \frac{5y^3-10y^2}{10y^2+70y} = \frac{y(y-2)}{2(y+7)}$$

Divide. Reduce your answer to lowest terms.

1. $\dfrac{3x}{y^3z^2} \div \dfrac{6y}{5x^3}$

2. $\dfrac{14m^3n}{3p^2} \div \dfrac{7m}{24p^4}$

3. $\dfrac{16y^5}{36y^3} \div \dfrac{9y^6}{4y^3}$

4. $\dfrac{x^2-81}{x^2+7x-18} \div \dfrac{-3x^3-3x^2}{x^2+2x+1}$

5. $\dfrac{\dfrac{-f-5}{15f+45}}{\dfrac{f^2+8f+15}{35}}$

6. $\dfrac{\dfrac{x^6}{x^9-2x^6}}{\dfrac{10x+20}{20}}$

Adding and Subtracting Rational Expressions

To add or subtract rational expressions, you must find the least common denominator.

Example:

$$\frac{4}{5e^3} - \frac{7+2e}{10e} \quad \text{The LCD}=10e^3 \quad \frac{4}{5e^3} \cdot \frac{2}{2} - \frac{(7+2e)}{10e} \cdot \frac{e^2}{e^2} =$$

$$\frac{8}{10e^3} + \frac{-7e^2 - 2e^3}{10e^3} = \frac{-2e^3 - 7e^2 + 8}{10e^3}$$

Add or subtract. Simplify if possible.

1. $\dfrac{7a}{3} - \dfrac{6a}{12}$

2. $\dfrac{8h}{8} - \dfrac{3h}{32}$

3. $\dfrac{4}{q} - \dfrac{6}{h}$

4. $\dfrac{4d-3}{8} - \dfrac{6d-6}{24}$

5. $\dfrac{-3d+8}{6d} - \dfrac{6d-6}{18d^2}$

6. $\dfrac{7d}{5} - \dfrac{6d}{20}$

7. $\dfrac{5e+4}{5f+5} - \dfrac{3e}{10f+10}$

8. $\dfrac{-5c+2}{9c+6} - \dfrac{3c+7}{36c^2 + 24c}$

Solving Equations with Rational Expressions

Example:

$$\frac{3}{y-2} + \frac{2y}{4-y^2} = \frac{5}{y+2} \qquad \frac{3}{y-2} + \frac{2y}{-(y-2)(y+2)} = \frac{5}{y+2}$$

$$\frac{3(y+2)}{(y-2)(y+2)} + \frac{-2y}{(y-2)(y+2)} = \frac{5(y-2)}{(y+2)(y-2)}$$

$$3(y+2) - 2y = 5(y-2)$$
$$3y + 6 - 2y = 5y - 10$$
$$y + 6 = 5y - 10$$
$$16 = 4y$$
$$\mathbf{y = 4}$$

Solve. Check your solution(s).

1. $\dfrac{x}{10} = \dfrac{2}{5} + \dfrac{3}{8}$

2. $\dfrac{3}{y} + \dfrac{7}{y} = 5$

3. $\dfrac{a-2}{a-4} = \dfrac{2}{a-4}$

4. $\dfrac{1}{2} - \dfrac{4}{9x} = \dfrac{4}{9} - \dfrac{1}{6x}$

5. $\dfrac{x}{x+2} - \dfrac{x}{x^2-4} = \dfrac{x+3}{x+2}$

6. $\dfrac{5}{c+3} = \dfrac{1}{4c^2-36} + \dfrac{2}{c-3}$

Simplifying Radicals

$$\sqrt[3]{\left(\frac{-64}{125}\right)} = \frac{\sqrt[3]{-64}}{\sqrt[3]{125}}$$

$$\sqrt[4]{48a^3b^5c}$$

$$= \frac{\sqrt[3]{-4 \cdot -4 \cdot -4}}{\sqrt[3]{5 \cdot 5 \cdot 5}}$$

$$= \sqrt[4]{2 \cdot 2 \cdot 2 \cdot 2 \cdot 3 \cdot a^3 \cdot b^4 \cdot b \cdot c}$$

$$= \frac{-4}{5}$$

$$= 2b\sqrt[4]{3a^3bc}$$

Simplify.

1. $\sqrt{4g^4d^3}$

2. $\sqrt{\frac{81}{16}}$

3. $\sqrt{49b^7e^3k^4}$

4. $\sqrt[4]{\frac{256}{16}}$

5. $-\sqrt[3]{1000f^3k^5d^8c^{11}}$

6. $\sqrt[3]{\frac{-200k^{11}}{27}}$

7. $-\sqrt[4]{81m^{14}j^9}$

8. $\sqrt[4]{\frac{625e^4}{1296}}$

9. $\sqrt[3]{\frac{-27f^9}{8f^6}}$

10. $\sqrt[5]{8(y-2)^6}$

Example:

$$\sqrt{3} - 2\sqrt{2} + 3\sqrt{8}$$
$$= \sqrt{3} - 2\sqrt{2} + 6\sqrt{2}$$
$$= \sqrt{3} + (-2 + 6)\sqrt{2}$$
$$= \mathbf{\sqrt{3} + 4\sqrt{2}}$$

$$\sqrt[4]{x^5} + 4x\sqrt[4]{16x}$$
$$= x\sqrt[4]{x} + (4 \bullet 2)x\sqrt[4]{x}$$
$$= (x + 8x)\sqrt[4]{x}$$
$$= \mathbf{9x\sqrt[4]{x}}$$

Simplify.

1. $\sqrt{3} - \sqrt{12} + \sqrt{27}$

2. $\sqrt{4} + \sqrt{16} - \sqrt{36}$

3. $2\sqrt{3} + \sqrt{11} - \sqrt{3} + 4\sqrt{11}$

4. $4\sqrt[3]{5} - 2\sqrt[3]{5} - \sqrt[3]{6} + 3\sqrt[3]{20}$

5. $-4\sqrt[3]{24} - 3\sqrt[3]{81} + 5\sqrt[3]{3}$

6. $\sqrt{27x} + 27 + 2\sqrt{3x} + 3$

7. $\sqrt[4]{2y} + 4\sqrt[4]{y^5} - 3y\sqrt[4]{y}$

8. $\sqrt{x^3} - 2x\sqrt{x} + 4\sqrt{x^4} - 2\sqrt{x^5}$

Multiplying Radicals

$$\sqrt{8x^3y^2 \cdot 10xy^3}$$
$$= \sqrt{80x^4y^5}$$
$$= \sqrt{2^4 \cdot 5 \cdot x^4y^5}$$
$$= 4x^2y^2\sqrt{5y}$$

$$(2 + \sqrt{3})(3 + \sqrt{6})$$
$$= 2(3) + 2(\sqrt{6}) + (\sqrt{3})(3) + (\sqrt{3})(\sqrt{6})$$
$$= 6 + 2\sqrt{6} + 3\sqrt{3} + \sqrt{18}$$
$$= 6 + 2\sqrt{6} + 3\sqrt{3} + 3\sqrt{2}$$

Simplify.

1. $\sqrt{4c^4d} \cdot \sqrt{8c^2e^3}$

2. $\sqrt{49bc} \cdot \sqrt{2b^2}$

3. $\sqrt[3]{x^5y^{15}} \cdot \sqrt[3]{x^2y^7}$

4. $\sqrt[3]{5xy} \cdot \sqrt[3]{15x^4y}$

5. $\sqrt{3(y + 2)^3} \cdot \sqrt{6(y + 2)^{17}}$

6. $(4x + \sqrt{3})(2x + \sqrt{3})$

7. $(1 + \sqrt{5y})(5 + \sqrt{4})$

8. $(8 + \sqrt{3})(8 - \sqrt{3})$

Example:

$$\frac{\sqrt{2x^3}}{\sqrt{3}} = \frac{x\sqrt{2x}}{\sqrt{3}} \cdot \frac{\sqrt{3}}{\sqrt{3}} = \frac{x\sqrt{6x}}{3}$$

$$\frac{5+\sqrt{3}}{4+\sqrt{3}} = \frac{5+\sqrt{3}}{4+\sqrt{3}} \cdot \frac{4-\sqrt{3}}{4-\sqrt{3}} = \frac{20-5\sqrt{3}+4\sqrt{3}-3}{16-4\sqrt{3}+4\sqrt{3}-3} = \frac{17-\sqrt{3}}{13}$$

conjugates

Divide and simplify.

1. $\dfrac{2}{\sqrt{5}}$

2. $\dfrac{\sqrt{6}}{\sqrt{3}}$

3. $\dfrac{\sqrt{3x}}{\sqrt{4x}}$

4. $\dfrac{\sqrt[3]{5}}{\sqrt[3]{3}}$

5. $\dfrac{5}{5-\sqrt{11}}$

6. $\dfrac{-3}{4-\sqrt{3}}$

7. $\dfrac{2+\sqrt{3}}{2-\sqrt{3}}$

8. $\dfrac{x+\sqrt{3}}{x+\sqrt{6}}$

Solving Equations with Radicals

Example:

$$3 + \sqrt[3]{2x} = 5$$
$$\sqrt[3]{2x} = 2$$
$$(\sqrt[3]{2x})^3 = (2)^3$$
$$2x = 8$$
$$\mathbf{x = 4}$$

Check:

$$3 + \sqrt[3]{2(4)} \overset{?}{=} 5$$
$$3 + \sqrt[3]{8} \overset{?}{=} 2$$
$$3 + 2 = 5 \checkmark$$

Solve. Check your solution.

1. $\sqrt{x} = 3$

2. $\sqrt{5y} = 5$

3. $\sqrt{2x - 3} = 4$

4. $\sqrt[3]{y} = -2$

5. $\sqrt[4]{x + 3} = -3$

6. $\sqrt[3]{2y + 1} + 5 = 0$

7. $\sqrt{3x + 1} = \sqrt{2x + 6}$

8. $3 + \sqrt{y - 6} = \sqrt{y + 9}$

Imaginary Numbers

i is called an imaginary number.

$$i = \sqrt{-1} \qquad\qquad i^2 = -1 \qquad\qquad i^3 = -i \qquad\qquad i^4 = 1$$

 **Example:**

$$
\begin{aligned}
i^{13} &= (i^4)^3 \cdot i \\
&= (1)^3 \cdot i \\
&= i
\end{aligned}
\qquad\qquad
\begin{aligned}
(i^2)^6 + i^5 &= i^{12} + i^5 \\
&= (i^4)^3 + (i^4)i \\
&= 1 + i
\end{aligned}
$$

1. i^5

2. i^{10}

3. i^6

4. i^{12}

5. i^{17}

6. $(i^{20})^3$

7. $i^{16} \cdot i^0$

8. $i^1 + i^{29}$

9. $\dfrac{i^{15}}{i^{14}}$

10. $(i^{11})^3 + i^3$

Complex Numbers

A complex number is in the form a + b*i*.

$$-2i + \sqrt{25} + \sqrt{-36} = -2i + \sqrt{25} + i\sqrt{36}$$
$$= -2i + 5 + i\sqrt{2^2 \cdot 3^2}$$
$$= -2i + 5 + 6i$$
$$= \mathbf{5 + 4i}$$

1. $\sqrt{60} - \sqrt{-48}$

2. $(2 + 4i) + (6 - 5i)$

3. $(12 - \sqrt{-50}) + (76 - \sqrt{-8})$

4. $(7i)(-6i)$

5. $(\sqrt{3})(\sqrt{-2} + \sqrt{3})$

6. $2i(6i + 2)$

7. $(4 - 3i)(4 + 3i)$

8. $i\sqrt{3}\,(\sqrt{12} - i\sqrt{6})$

9. $(4 - 7i)(2 + 5i)$

10. $(8 - \sqrt{-4}) - (2 + \sqrt{-36})$

Rational Exponents

$$\sqrt[n]{a} = a^{1/n} \quad \text{and} \quad \sqrt[n]{a^m} = a^{m/n}$$

Example:

$$\sqrt[4]{(2a)^3} = (2a)^{3/4} \qquad \left(\frac{2r}{7s}\right)^{-5/2} = \left(\frac{7s}{2r}\right)^{5/2} \qquad (a^{-1/2}b^{3/4})^{1/3} = a^{(-1/2)(1/3)}b^{(3/4)(1/3)}$$
$$= a^{-1/6}b^{1/4}$$
$$= \frac{b^{1/4}}{a^{1/6}}$$

Simplify. Rewrite with positive, rational exponents.

1. $\sqrt[3]{x^2}$

2. $\sqrt[5]{xy^2z^3}$

3. $\left(\frac{3a}{4b}\right)^{-3/5}$

4. $\left(\sqrt[8]{6^3}\right)^{2/7}$

5. $2^{1/4} \cdot 2^{2/5}$

6. $x^{1/7} \cdot x^{3/7} \cdot x^{2/7}$

7. $g^{2/3} \cdot g^{5/4}$

8. $(x^{-1/3} y^{-2/5})^{-15}$

9. $\dfrac{c^{-4/5} d^{5/9}}{c^{7/10} d^{1/6}}$

10. $\sqrt[3]{\sqrt{xy}}$

Factoring Quadratic Equations

The standard form of a quadratic equation is: $ax^2 + bx + c = 0$
(where a, b, c are real numbers and $a \neq 0$)

$6x^2 - 7x = 3$

$6x^2 - 7x - 3 = 0$ Write in standard form.

$(3x + 1)(2x - 3) = 0$ Factor.

$3x + 1 = 0$ $2x - 3 = 0$ Let each product equal 0.

$x = -\frac{1}{3}$ or $x = \frac{3}{2}$ Solve.

Solve by factoring.

1. $a^2 + 3a = 28$

2. $2x^2 - 7x - 4 = 0$

3. $9y^2 - 3 = -6y$

4. $y^2 - 16 = 0$

5. $32 + 4x - x^2 = 0$

6. $6d - d^2 = 0$

7. $7c^2 - 7 = 0$

8. $2f^3 - 2f^2 = 12f$

Example:

$$3(x + 4)^2 = -12$$
$$(x + 4)^2 = -4$$
$$\sqrt{(x + 4)^2} = \sqrt{-4}$$
$$x + 4 = \pm 2i$$ Note: If $a^2 = k$, then $a = \pm\sqrt{k}$.
$$x = -4 \pm 2i$$

Solve by taking square roots.

1. $y^2 = 81$

2. $w^2 - 4 = 0$

3. $9e^2 - 16 = 0$

4. $(u + 2)^2 = 25$

5. $5(p + 2)^2 = 125$

6. $(s - 2)^2 + 4 = 0$

7. $(g + \frac{2}{3})^2 = 1/9$

8. $8(z + \frac{1}{2})^2 + 40 = 0$

Completing the Square

Example:

$2x^2 + 24x + 23 = 0$ Does not factor.

$x^2 + 12x + \dfrac{23}{2} = 0$ Make coefficient of x^2 a 1.

$x^2 + 12x = -\dfrac{23}{2}$ Add $-\dfrac{23}{2}$ to both sides.

$x^2 + 12x + 36 = -\dfrac{23}{2} + 36$ Take half of 12 (coefficient of x), and square it. Add to both sides.

$(x + 6)^2 = \dfrac{49}{2}$ Factor.

$\sqrt{(x + 6)^2} = \sqrt{\dfrac{49}{2}}$

$x + 6 = \dfrac{7}{\sqrt{2}}$

$\mathbf{x = -6 + \dfrac{7\sqrt{2}}{2}}$ Rationalize the denominator.

Solve by completing the square.

1. $j^2 + 12j + 4 = 0$ **2.** $k^2 - 8k = 9$

3. $2n^2 - 8n - 14 = 0$ **4.** $b^2 - 9b + 25 = 0$

5. $4v^2 + 4v = 3$ **6.** $x^2 = 4\sqrt{3}x - 12$

        Algebra II Grades 6–8—RBP0830

The Quadratic Formula

If an equation is of the form $ax^2 + bx + c = 0$, then the quadratic equation to solve for x is: $\dfrac{-b \pm \sqrt{b^2 - 4ac}}{2a}$

$2x^2 + 6x + 18 = 0$ $a = 2, b = 6, c = 18$

$x = \dfrac{-6 \pm \sqrt{6^2 - 4(2)(18)}}{2(2)}$ $= \dfrac{-6 \pm \sqrt{36 - 144}}{4}$ $= \dfrac{-6 \pm \sqrt{-108}}{4}$

$= \dfrac{-6 \pm 6i\sqrt{3}}{4}$ $= \dfrac{-3 \pm 3i\sqrt{3}}{2}$

Solve using the quadratic equation.

1. $4x^2 - 5x + 1 = 0$

2. $x^2 - 6x + 4 = 0$

3. $5y^2 + 4 = -3y$

4. $z^2 + 3z = -8$

5. $5q^2 - 46q = -48$

6. $4w^2 = 9w - 3$

Graphing Quadratic Equations Using a Table

Graph $y = x^2 - 2x - 3$.

Graph using a table.

Pick at least four points.

Plot until you visualize the parabola.

x	$x^2 - 2x - 3$	y
-4	$16 + 8 - 3$	21
-2	$4 + 4 - 3$	5
0	$0 - 0 - 3$	-3
2	$4 - 4 - 3$	-3
4	$16 - 8 - 3$	5

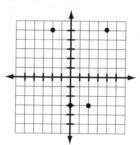

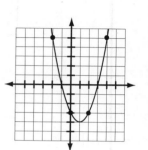

Graph using a table of ordered pairs.

1. $y = x^2 - x - 3$

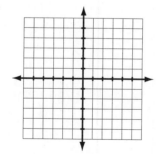

2. $y = 2x^2 + 4x + 1$

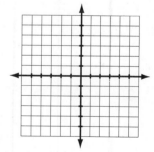

3. $y = x^2 + 2$

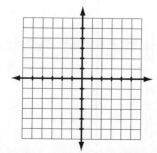

4. $y = -x^2 - 4x + 2$

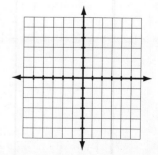

Algebra II Grades 6–8—RBP0830

Finding X-Intercepts of
Quadratic Equations

 **Example:**

To find the x-intercepts of $y = 2x^2 - 6x - 10$:

1. Let y = 0.

$$0 = 2x^2 - 6x - 10$$

2. Solve for x.

$$x = \frac{6 \pm \sqrt{36 - 4(2)(-10)}}{2(2)}$$

$$x = \frac{6 \pm \sqrt{36 + 80}}{4} = \frac{6 \pm \sqrt{116}}{4}$$

$$x = \frac{6 \pm 2\sqrt{29}}{4} = \frac{3 \pm \sqrt{29}}{2}$$

$$\approx \textbf{4.19 or -1.19}$$

Solve using the quadratic equation.

1. $y = x^2 - 3x - 18$

2. $y = x^2 - 32$

3. $y = x^2 - 6x$

4. $y = 5(3x - 8)^2 - 10$

5. $y = 2x^2 + 2x - 2$

6. $y = 3x^2 - 15x - 20$

The axis of symmetry and vertex of a quadratic equation can be found using: $x = -\dfrac{b}{2a}$

Find the axis of symmetry and vertex of $y = 2x^2 - 8x - 10$.

1. Use $x = -\dfrac{b}{2a}$ to find the value of x: $x = \dfrac{-(-8)}{2(2)} = \dfrac{8}{4} = 2$

    This is the axis of symmetry: **x = 2**

2. To find y, substitute x into equation.
    $y = 2(2)^2 - 8(2) - 10$
    $y = 8 - 16 - 10$
    y = -18

    The vertex is: **(2,-18)**

Find the vertex.

1. $y = -2x^2 - 4x$

2. $y = -x^2 + 2x$

3. $y = x^2 - x - 6$

4. $y = x^2 + 8x + 16$

5. $y = x^2 + 2x + 4$

6. $y = 5x^2 - 12x - 20$

Graphing Using X-Intercepts and Vertex

Graph $y = 4x^2 + 10x + 1$.

Find the x-intercepts:

$0 = 4x^2 + 10x + 1$

$x = \dfrac{-10 \pm \sqrt{100 - 16}}{8}$

$x = \dfrac{-10 \pm 2\sqrt{21}}{8}$

$x \approx \dfrac{-5 \pm \sqrt{21}}{4}$

$\approx -.10, -2.40$

Find the vertex:

$x = -\dfrac{b}{2a} = -\dfrac{10}{8} = -\dfrac{5}{4} = -1.25$

$y = 4(\dfrac{25}{16}) + 10(\dfrac{-5}{4}) + 1$

$= \dfrac{-21}{4}$

$= -5.25$

$(-1.25, -5.25)$

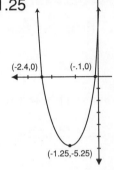

Graph using x-intercepts and vertex.

1. $y = -x^2 - 4x + 2$

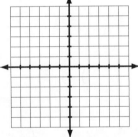

2. $y = x^2 + 8x + 12$

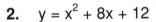
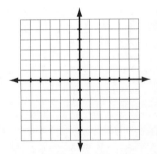

3. $y = 4x^2 + 12x + 7$

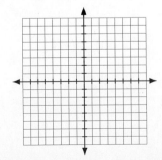

4. $y = 2x^2 - 12x + 10$

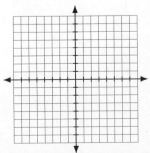

Finding Values of Functions

A function is a correspondence from one set to another.
f(x) is read "f of x". It does <u>not</u> mean f times x.

Example:

Find $f(x) = 5x^2 - 3x + 1$ for the given value of x.

$$f(-7) = 5(-7)^2 - 3(-7) + 1$$
$$= 5(49) + 21 + 1$$
$$= 245 + 21 + 1$$
$$= 267$$

$$f(5a) = 5(5a)^2 - 3(5a) + 1$$
$$= 125a^2 - 15a + 1$$

Find the following function values.

1. If $f(x) = 11x + 8x^2$

   a) f(-6)   b) f(2)   c f(-3)   d) f(1)

2. If $g(x) = x^3$

   a) g(-1)   b) g(4)   c) g(-5)   d) g(2m)

3. If $h(x) = |x| + 2$

   a) h(5)   b) h(-4)   c) h(-14)   d) $h(x^2)$

Domain and Range

Domain is the set of x values for a given function.
Range is the set of y values for a given function.

Example:

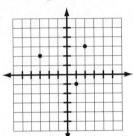

Domain: {-3, 1, 2}
Range: {-1, 2, 3}

Domain: all reals
Range: y ≥ 1

Find the domain and range of the following functions.

1.

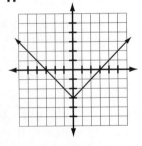

_____

_____

2.

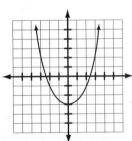

_____

_____

3.

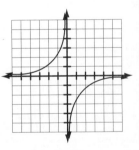

_____

_____

4.

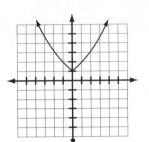

_____

_____

5.

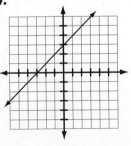

_____

_____

6.

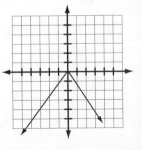

_____

_____

Composite Functions

Example:

If $f(x) = x + 3$ and $g(x) = 2x^2$

Find $f(g(x))$.
$f(g(x)) = f(2x^2)$
$\qquad = 2x^2 + 3$

Find $g(f(x))$.
$g(f(x)) = g(x + 3)$
$\qquad = 2(x + 3)^2$
$\qquad = 2(x^2 + 6x + 9)$
$\qquad = 2x^2 + 12x + 18$

$f(x) = 3x - 5$ $\qquad\qquad$ $g(x) = x^2 - 1$ $\qquad\qquad$ $h(x) = x + 3$

Find the composition of the following functions.

1. $f(g(x))$

2. $g(h(x))$

3. $h(f(x))$

4. $g(f(x))$

5. $f(h(x))$

6. $f(h(g(x)))$

39

Algebra II Grades 6–8—RBP0830

If f(x) = 3x + 4 and g(x) = x – 1

Find (f ° g)(x).   Find g(x) – f(x).
Note: ° means multiply
(f ° g)(x) = (3x + 4)(x – 1)   g(x) – f(x) = x – 1 – (3x + 4)
        = **3x² + x – 4**   = x – 1 – 3x – 4
                                    = **-2x – 5**

Find the composition of the following functions.

$f(x) = 5x - 1$ $g(x) = x^2 - 2$ $h(x) = 3x$

1. (f ° g)(x)   **2.** g(x) + h(x)

3. (g ° h)(x)   **4.** f(x) – g(x)

5. (f ° g)(3)   **6.** (g ° h)(-3)

One-to-One Functions

A function must pass the vertical line test.
A 1-1 function passes both a vertical and a horizontal line test.

Example:

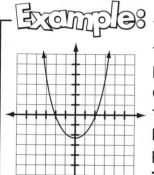

This graph passes the vertical line test because on any vertical line drawn, the graph only passes through the line once or not at all.

This graph does not pass the horizontal test because a horizontal line can be drawn that passes through more than one point.

The graph is a function, but not 1-1.

Determine whether each graph is a function and 1-1.

1.

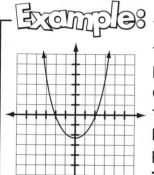

_____

_____

2.

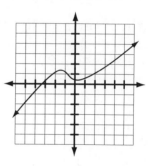

_____

_____

3.

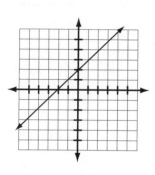

_____

_____

4.

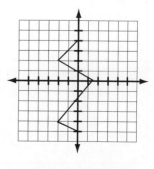

_____

_____

Inverse Functions

A function f has an inverse only if the function f is one-to-one. (It passes the vertical and horizontal line tests.)
The inverse function is denoted as f^{-1}.

Find the inverse of $f(x) = 2x + 8$.

1. Replace f(x) with y. $y = 2x + 8$
2. Interchange x and y. $x = 2y + 8$
3. Solve for y. $x - 8 = 2y$

$$\frac{x}{2} - 4 = y$$

$$f^{-1}(x) = \frac{x}{2} - 4$$

Find the inverse of the following functions.

1. $f(x) = 4x - 8$

2. $f(x) = 3x + 6$

3. $f(x) = \frac{x}{2} - 1$

4. $f(x) = (\frac{2}{3})x + 4$

5. $f(x) = \frac{4}{5x} - 3$

6. $f(x) = x^3$

Example:

Solve $125 = 25^x$.

1. Get same bases. $125 = 5^3$ and $25 = 5^2$. $5^3 = (5^2)^x$

2. Set exponents equal to each other. $3 = 2x$

3. Solve. $\dfrac{3}{2} = x$

Solve.

1. $2^x = 8$

2. $9^x = 27$

3. $4^x = \dfrac{1}{16}$

4. $4^{3t} = 64$

5. $9^{4y} = \dfrac{1}{81}$

6. $3^{3x-1} = 9^{x-1}$

7. $5^{2x-2} = 25^{2x+5}$

8. $9^{2-x} = 27^{x/3}$

    Algebra II Grades 6–8—RBP0830

Converting Logarithmic and Exponential Forms

$y = \log_b x$ is equivalent to $x = b^y$.

Example:

Write $6^x = 216$ in logarithmic form. $\mathbf{x = \log_6 216}$

Write $\log_5 625 = x$ in exponential form. $\mathbf{5^x = 625}$

Write problems 1–5 in logarithmic form. Write problems 6–10 in exponential form.

1. $3^4 = 81$

2. $10^{-1} = 0.1$

3. $8^{-1/3} = \dfrac{1}{2}$

4. $10^4 = 10000$

5. $15^{5/2} = 225\sqrt{15}$

6. $\log_2 8 = 3$

7. $\log_5 125 = 3$

8. $\log_3 \dfrac{1}{27} = -3$

9. $\log_{3.2} 3.2 = 1$

10. $\log_{2/3} \dfrac{27}{8} = -3$

44

Solving Logarithmic Equations

Example:

$$\log_4 \frac{1}{4} = \frac{x}{64}$$

1. Rewrite in exponential notation. $4^{x/64} = \frac{1}{4}$

2. Write with common base. $4^{x/64} = 4^{-1}$

3. Set exponents equal to each other. $\frac{x}{64} = -1$

4. Solve.   **x = -64**

Solve.

1. $\log_x 25 = 2$

2. $\log_{10} x = 3$

3. $\log_x 3 = \frac{1}{2}$

4. $\log_3 27 = 3x + 6$

5. $\log_7 \frac{1}{49} = -x - 4$

6. $\log_{1/10} 100 = x$

7. $\log_{2/3} \frac{4}{9} = 2x$

8. $\log_{1/3} 9 = x + 3$

A common logarithm is a log with base = 10.

$$\log A = \log_{10} A$$

A natural logarithm (ln) is a log with base e.

(e is used in many applications.)

$$\ln x = \log_e x$$

Both log and ln keys can be found on a scientific calculator.

Example:

Find log 0.08 using a calculator.

$\log 0.05 \approx$ **-1.097**

Find ln 5.2 using a calculator.

$\ln 5.2 \approx$ **1.649**

Solve. Round answers to the nearest thousandth.

1. log 3.7

2. log 322

3. log 0.05

4. log 2 + log 6

5. $\dfrac{\log 151}{\log 9}$

6. ln 4.5

7. ln 62

8. ln 640

9. ln 1000 + ln 500

10. $\dfrac{\ln 24}{\ln 2}$

Evaluating Common and Natural Logarithms

If log A = y then $\log_{10}A$ = y and 10^y = A.
If ln x = y then $\log_e x$ = y and e^y = x.

Use the 10^x and e^x keys found on a scientific calculator to find the following.

	log x = 0.02			ln x = 5.2
1. Rewrite.	$10^{0.02}$ = x		**1.** Rewrite.	$e^{5.2}$ = x
2. Solve.	**1.047 = x**		**2.** Solve.	**181.272 = x**

Use a calculator to solve for x. Round answers to the nearest thousandth.

1. log x = 3.963

2. log x = 0.0238

3. log x = -0.3421

4. log x = -0.98

5. ln x = 1.304

6. ln x = 8.628

7. ln x = 0.0832

8. ln x = -5.2

47

Change of Base Formula

$$\log_b x = \frac{\log_c x}{\log_c b} = \frac{\ln x}{\ln b}$$

(where $b > 0$ and $b \neq 1$)

 **Example:**

Calculate $\log_3 7$.

$$\log_3 7 = \frac{\ln 7}{\ln 3}$$

$$\approx \frac{1.946}{1.099}$$

$$\approx \mathbf{1.771}$$

Use a calculator to find each logarithm to the nearest thousandth.

1. $\log_4 3.7$

2. $\log_5 25$

3. $\log_3 22$

4. $\log_{14} 0.05$

5. $\log_2 2$

6. $\log_{10} 6$

7. $\log_{0.5} 51$

8. $\dfrac{\log_9 153}{\log_4 52}$

9. $\log_3 2 + \log_3 5$

10. $5 \log_6 98 - 4 \log_5 16$

Using Logarithms to Solve Exponential Equations

Example:

$3^{x+1} = 48.2$

Rewrite using logs. $\log_3 48.2 = x + 1$

Use change of base formula. $\dfrac{\ln 48.2}{\ln 3} = x + 1$

Evaluate. $\dfrac{3.875}{1.099} \approx x + 1$

                                       $3.53 \approx x + 1$

                                       $3.53 - 1 \approx x$

                                       $\mathbf{x \approx 2.53}$

Solve for x. Round answers to nearest hundredth.

1. $6^{2x} = 123$

2. $1.2^x = 6$

3. $4^{2x-1} = 53.2$

4. $5^{4x} = 61.5$

5. $5^{2x+3} = 52.1$

6. $1.2^{2x} - 12 = 68$

Algebra II Grades 6–8—RBP0830

$$\log_b uv = \log_b u + \log_b v$$

$$\log_b \frac{u}{v} = \log_b u - \log_b v$$

$$\log_b u^n = n \cdot \log_b u$$

Example:

Write $\log_a x^2 y$ in expanded form.

$\log_a x^2 y = \log_a x^2 + \log_a y$

$\qquad = \mathbf{2\log_a x + \log_a y}$

Write $4\log_2 x - \log_2 y$ as a single logarithm.

$4\log_2 x - \log_2 y = \log_2 x^4 - \log_2 y$

$$= \mathbf{\log_2 \frac{x^4}{y}}$$

Express 1–5 in expanded form. Express 6–10 as a single logarithm.

1. $\log_4 3y$

2. $\log_a \frac{b}{c}$

3. $\log_4 \sqrt{5}$

4. $\log_5 2x^3$

5. $\log_b (\frac{x}{5})^{2y}$

6. $\log_4 x + \log_4 y + \log_4 z$

7. $5\log_2 m + \log_2 n$

8. $\frac{1}{2}\log_3 x - \log_3 y$

9. $\log_3 a - \frac{1}{4}\log_3 b$

10. $(\log_4 x + \log_4 y) - \log_4 z$

Solving Equations Using Properties of Logarithms

Example:

$\log_3 x + \log_3(x - 6) = 3$

$\log_3 x(x - 6) = 3$

$3^3 = x(x - 6)$

$27 = x^2 - 6x$

$x^2 - 6x - 27 = 0$

$(x + 3)(x - 9) = 0$

$x = \mathbf{-3}$ or $x = \mathbf{9}$

Check:

-3 is not a solution since $\log_3(-3)$ is undefined.

$\log_3 9 + \log_3(9 - 6) \overset{?}{=} 3$

$\log_3 9 + \log_3 3 \overset{?}{=} 3$

$\log_3(9 \cdot 3) \overset{?}{=} 3$

$\log_3 27 \overset{?}{=} 3$

$3^3 = 27$ ✔

Solve for x. Check your solution(s).

1. $\log_3 3x + \log_3 9x = 4$

2. $\log_y x = 4\log_y 2 - \log_y 2$

3. $\log_2(x+7) + \log_2 x = 3$

4. $\log_{12} 6x + \log_{12} 4x = 2$

5. $\log_3(x^2 - 22) = 3$

6. $\log_5(x + 1) - \log_5 7 = \log_5(x - 1)$

Example:

Graph $f(x) = (\frac{3}{4})^{x+1}$.

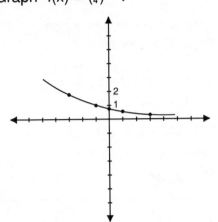

x	$(\frac{3}{4})^{x+1}$	f(x)
0	$(\frac{3}{4})^1$	.75
1	$(\frac{3}{4})^2$	$\frac{9}{16} \approx .56$
-1	$(\frac{3}{4})^0$	1
3	$(\frac{3}{4})^4$	$\frac{81}{256} \approx .32$
-3	$(\frac{3}{4})^{-2}$	$\frac{16}{9} \approx 1.78$

Graph the following functions.

1. $f(x) = 2^x$

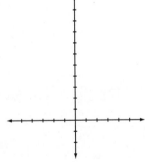

2. $f(x) = (\frac{1}{5})^x$

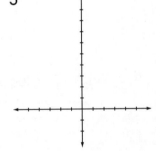

3. $f(x) = 2^{x+1}$

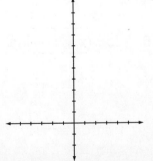

4. $f(x) = 3^{x-2}$

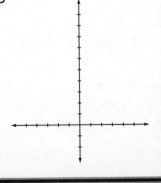

Graph the following functions.

1. $f(x) = 3^x$

2. $f(x) = 6^x$

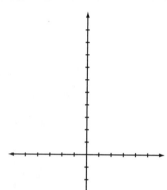

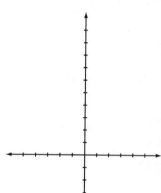

3. $f(x) = (\frac{1}{2})^x$

4. $f(x) = (\frac{1}{4})^x$

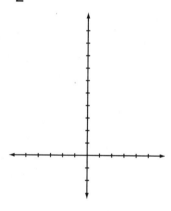

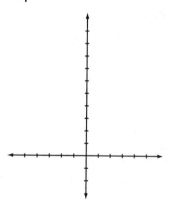

What do you think will happen to a graph if the base is increased?

_____

_____

What do you notice about the graph if the base is less than 1?

_____

_____

Algebra II Grades 6–8—RBP0830

Graphing Logarithmic Functions

Logarithmic functions are the inverse of exponential functions.

Example:

Graph f(x) = log4x.

1. Rewrite. If y=$\log_4 x$, then 4^y = x

2. Pick y values and solve for x.

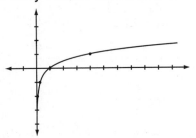

x = 4^y	y
1	0
$\frac{1}{4}$	-1
4	1
16	2
$\frac{1}{16}$	-2

Graph the following functions.

1. f(x) = $\log_5 x$

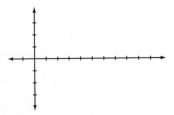

2. f(x) = $\log_{1/2} x$

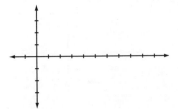

3. f(x) = $\log_2 x$

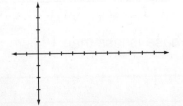

4. f(x) = $\log_{1/4} x$

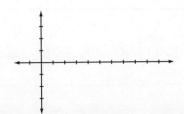

Parabolas

Review how to graph parabolas on pages 33–36.

Parabolas can also have a line of symmetry along the x-axis. The standard form for these parabolas is: $x = ay^2 + by + c$

Example:

$$x = -2y^2 + 10y - 7$$

1. Find the vertex using $y = \dfrac{-b}{2a}$. $\quad y = \dfrac{-10}{2(-2)} = \dfrac{-10}{-4} = \dfrac{5}{2}$

2. Find the x coordinate of vertex. $\quad x = -2(\dfrac{5}{2})^2 + 10(\dfrac{5}{2}) - 7 = \dfrac{11}{2}$

The vertex is $(\dfrac{11}{2}, \dfrac{5}{2})$.

3. Find ordered pairs (picking y values) to determine the shape of the parabola.

We will pick 5, 3, 1, 0.

y	$x = -2y^2 + 10y - 7$	x
5	x = -2(25) + 10(5) − 7	-7
3	x = -2(9) + 10(3) − 7	5
1	x = -2(1) + 10(1) − 7	1
0	x = -2(0) + 10(0) − 7	-7

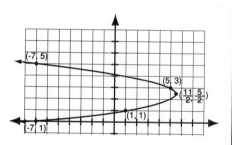

Graph the following functions.

1. $x = -3y^2 - 6y - 1$

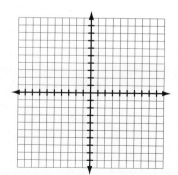

2. $x = 4 - 3y - y^2$

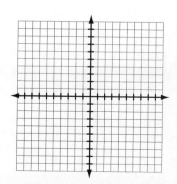

Algebra II Grades 6–8—RBP0830

Distance Formula

To find the distance between two points (x_1, y_1) and (x_2, y_2), use:

Distance$^2 = (x_2 - x_1)^2 + (y_2 - y_1)^2$

Find the distance between (4,2) and (2,-4).

$$D^2 = (2 - 4)^2 + (-4 - 2)^2$$
$$D^2 = (-2)^2 + (-6)^2$$
$$D^2 = 4 + 36$$
$$D^2 = 40$$
$$D = \sqrt{40} = 2\sqrt{10}$$

Find the distance between the given points.

1. (-5,-3), (-1,-3)

2. (-3,4), (-3,-6)

3. (4,5), (-2,-7)

4. (-6,-8), (1,6)

5. (4,8), (3,9)

6. (-4,7), (2,5)

7. (-3,-4), (-8,-9)

8. (6,2), (2,4)

Equation of a Circle

The standard form of an equation of a circle with a center at (h,k) and radius r is:

$$(x - h)^2 + (y - k)^2 = r^2$$

Find the center and radius of the circle with the equation $x^2 + y^2 - 6x - 4y - 10 = 0$.

1. Group terms. $(x^2 - 6x + \underline{}) + (y^2 - 4y + \underline{}) = 10$

2. Complete the square. $(x^2 - 6x + \mathbf{9}) + (y^2 - 4y + \mathbf{4}) = 10 \mathbf{+ 9 + 4}$

3. Write as squares. $(x - 3)^2 + (y - 2)^2 = 23$

The center is (3, 2) and radius is $\sqrt{23}$.

Find the center and radius of the circles with the following equations. Leave radius in reduced root form, if needed.

1. $(x - 2)^2 + (y + 3)^2 = 3^2$ **2.** $x^2 + y^2 - 8x - 12y - 3 = 0$

3. $(x - 5)^2 + (y - 4)^2 = 16$ **4.** $x^2 + y^2 + 7x - 8y = -5$

5. $x^2 + (y - 1)^2 = 36$ **6.** $x^2 + y^2 + 10x + 7 = 0$

Example:

Graph $x^2 + (y - 3)^2 = 25$ using center and radius.

The center is (0,3), and the radius is 5.

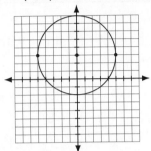

Graph the following equations of circles using center and radius.

1. $(x - 2)^2 + (y + 3)^2 = 3^2$

2. $(x - 1)^2 + (y + 1)^2 = 16$

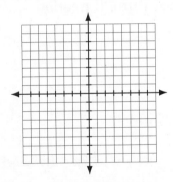
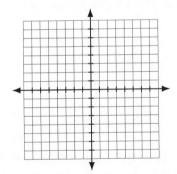

3. $x^2 + y^2 - 2y + 1 = 36$

4. $x^2 + y^2 + 4x - 6y = 3$

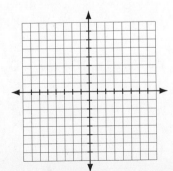
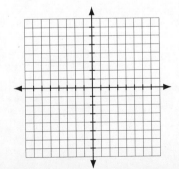

The standard form of an ellipse centered at (0,0) is

$$\frac{x^2}{a^2} + \frac{y^2}{b^2} = 1$$

where the x-intercepts are (a,0) and (-a,0) and the y-intercepts are (0,b) and (0,-b).

Sketch a graph of $\frac{x^2}{4} + \frac{y^2}{13} = 1$.

The x-intercepts are ±2 and the y-intercepts are ± $\sqrt{13}$ ≈ ± 3.6.

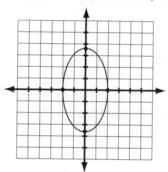

Sketch a graph of the ellipse given by the equation.

1. $\frac{x^2}{4} + \frac{y^2}{25} = 1$ **2.** $\frac{x^2}{20} + \frac{y^2}{9} = 1$

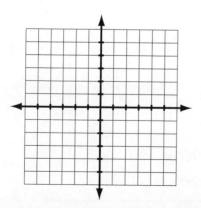   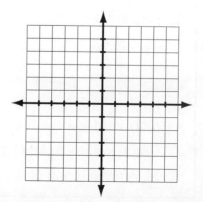

Algebra II Grades 6–8—RBP0830

Graphing Hyperbolas

The standard forms of hyperbolas centered at (0,0) are:

Form	Axis of Symmetry	Vertices
$\dfrac{x^2}{a^2} - \dfrac{y^2}{b^2} = 1$	x-axis	(a,0) and (-a,0)
$\dfrac{y^2}{b^2} - \dfrac{x^2}{a^2} = 1$	y-axis	(0,b) and (0,-b)

The asymptotes are the lines:

$y = (\dfrac{b}{a})x$ and $y = -(\dfrac{b}{a})x$

In the first graph, the axis of symmetry is the x-axis, and the vertices are x-intercepts.

In the second graph, the axis of symmetry is the y-axis, and the vertices are y-intercepts.

Notice that the hyperbola gets very close to, but never touches, either asymptote.

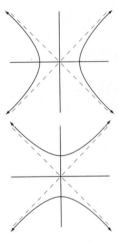

Example:

Sketch a graph of $\dfrac{y^2}{16} - \dfrac{x^2}{4} = 1$.

1. Identify axis of symmetry.
   y-axis

2. Identify a and b.
   a = 2   b = 4

3. Find the asymptotes.
   $y = (\dfrac{4}{2})x$ $y = (\dfrac{-4}{2})x$
   $y = 2x$ $y = -2x$

4. Find the vertices.
   (0,4)   (0,-4)

5. Graph the asymptotes and vertices.

6. Sketch the graph of the hyperbola.

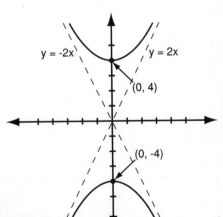

Graphing Hyperbolas

Sketch a graph of the hyperbola given by the equation.

1. $\dfrac{x^2}{16} - \dfrac{y^2}{4} = 1$

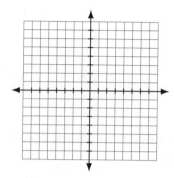

2. $\dfrac{x^2}{9} - \dfrac{y^2}{9} = 1$

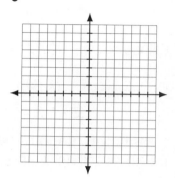

3. $\dfrac{y^2}{36} - \dfrac{x^2}{4} = 1$

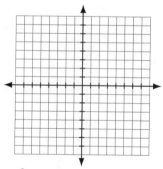

4. $\dfrac{x^2}{4} - \dfrac{y^2}{9} = 1$

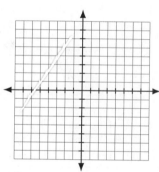

5. $\dfrac{y^2}{1} - \dfrac{x^2}{4} = 1$

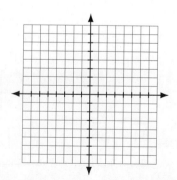

6. $\dfrac{y^2}{25} - \dfrac{x^2}{25} = 1$

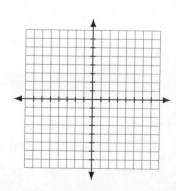

Algebra II Grades 6–8—RBP0830

Recognizing Conics

Type	Standard Equation(s)
Parabola	$y = ax^2 + bx + c$ or $x = ay^2 + by + c$
Circle	$(x - h)^2 + (y - k)^2 = r^2$
Ellipse	$\dfrac{(x - h)^2}{a^2} + \dfrac{(y - k)^2}{b^2} = 1$
Hyperbola	$\dfrac{(x - h)^2}{a^2} - \dfrac{(y - k)^2}{b^2} = 1$ or $\dfrac{(y - k)^2}{b^2} - \dfrac{(x - h)^2}{a^2} = 1$

Classify the graph of each of the following equations as a parabola, circle, ellipse, or hyperbola.

1. $x = \dfrac{-1y^2}{12}$

_____

2. $\dfrac{(x - 6)^2}{81} + \dfrac{(y + 2)^2}{49} = 1$

_____

3. $x + 6 = \dfrac{-1}{8}(y + 2)^2$

_____

4. $x^2 + y^2 = 4$

_____

5. $\dfrac{x^2}{4} + \dfrac{y^2}{16} = 1$

_____

6. $x - 9 = (y - 1)^2$

_____

7. $\dfrac{(x + 5)^2}{4} - \dfrac{(y - 3)^2}{64} = 1$

_____

8. $x^2 = 9 - y^2$

_____

9. $\dfrac{(y + 7)^2}{36} - \dfrac{(x + 8)^2}{1} = 1$

_____

10. $\dfrac{(y - 5)^2}{9} - \dfrac{(x + 4)^2}{9} = 1$

_____

11. $\dfrac{x^2}{9} + \dfrac{y^2}{49} = 1$

_____

12. $\dfrac{x^2}{64} - \dfrac{y^2}{36} = 1$

_____

Graphing Conics

Match the following equations with their graphs.

1. $(x - 1)^2 + y^2 = \dfrac{81}{4}$

a.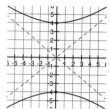

2. $\dfrac{x^2}{4} - \dfrac{y^2}{4} = 1$

b.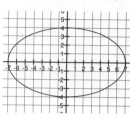

3. $y - 3 = \dfrac{-1}{4}(x - 3)^2$

c.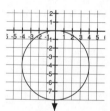

4. $\dfrac{x^2}{49} + \dfrac{y^2}{16} = 1$

d.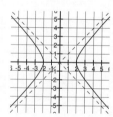

5. $x^2 + (y + 4)^2 = 16$

e.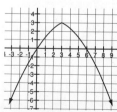

6. $\dfrac{y^2}{16} - \dfrac{x^2}{25} = 1$

f.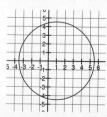

Example:

Find the solution(s) to the following system by graphing:

$$\frac{x^2}{4} + \frac{y^2}{16} = 1$$

$$\frac{x^2}{4} - \frac{y^2}{9} = 1$$

The solutions are **(-2,0)** and **(2,0)**.

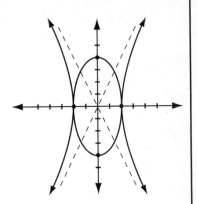

Graph the following systems. Find their solution(s) if any.

1. $\frac{x^2}{16} + \frac{y^2}{4} = 1$

$x^2 + y^2 = 16$

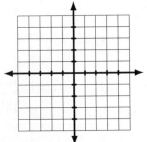

2. $x^2 + y^2 = 25$

$x - y = -5$

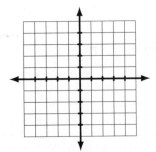

3. $x^2 + y^2 = 9$

$x^2 + y^2 = 4$

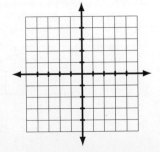

4. $2x - y = 4$

$x = \frac{y^2}{4}$

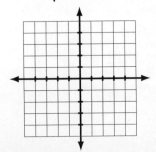

Mixtures

Solve by writing two equations and using substitution or elimination.

1. LaToya has $6.70 in nickels and dimes. If she has a total of 100 coins, how many of each does she have?

2. A store makes a mixture of cashews and peanuts. They want to mix 15 pounds of cashews that sell for $5.25 per pound with peanuts that sell for $2.50 per pound. How many pounds of peanuts should be added to the 15 pounds of cashews to obtain a blend that will sell for $3.75 per pound?

3. Lacey has 5 cups of a 70% salt solution. How many cups of 45% salt solution should she add to obtain a solution that is 55% salt?

4. Jose owed a total of $2100 on his two credit cards for one year. He paid $355.44 in interest. The rate charged by one card was 14% and the rate charged by the other card was 18%. How much did he owe on each card?

5. Caylee divided $124 between a savings account and a mutual fund. The savings account paid 4% in interest and the mutual fund paid 8% in interest. If she earned $8.24 in interest, how much did she put in each account?

Algebra II Grades 6–8—RBP0830

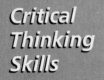
Motion

Use the formula d = rt (distance = rate • time) to solve the following. Use a table to help you write equation(s) to solve.

1. A car travels at a constant rate of 65 mph from Georgetown to Franklin. A second car starts out at the same point but leaves an hour later at a constant rate of 75 mph. How long will the second car be driving before it catches up to the first car?

2. A train leaves Salt Lake City traveling west at 40 mph. One hour later, another train leaves Salt Lake City, also traveling west, but at 70 mph. How far from Salt Lake will they be when the faster train catches up with the slower one?

3. A plane flew for 8 hours with a 20 mph tailwind. The return flight against the same wind took 10 hours. Find the speed of the plane in still air.

4. Two cars leave Chicago traveling in opposite directions. One car travels at a speed of 60 mph and the other at 52 mph. In how many hours will they be 504 miles apart?

5. A boat travels 1 $\frac{1}{2}$ hours downstream with a 6-mph current. The return trip takes 4 hours. Find the speed of the boat in still water.

Average Rate and Work

Use rational equations to solve the following.

1. Justin drove from his home to Atlanta at an average speed of 40 mph. He returned home traveling the same route at an average speed of 45 mph. What is his average speed for the entire trip?

2. Madison drove from her home to her office at an average speed of 65 mph. She returned to her home traveling the same route at an average speed of 40 mph. What was her average speed for the entire trip?

3. Rauel drove his car in rush hour traffic from his office to his home at an average speed of 40 mph. Taking the same route back he averaged 60 mph. What was his average speed for the entire trip?

4. A carpenter can build a cedar chest in 10 hours. (He can complete $\frac{1}{10}$ of the chest in one hour). A second carpenter can build the same chest in 15 hours. How long will it take them to build the chest if they work together?

5. A head janitor can completely clean a school in 12 hours. Another janitor can do the same job in 16 hours. After working alone for 4 hours, the head janitor leaves and the other janitor finishes cleaning the school. How long will it take the second janitor to finish cleaning the school?

Pythagorean Theorem

Use $a^2 + b^2 = c^2$ to help solve the following problems.

1. Jack and Joyce are planting a garden. They have a 40-foot by 30-foot rectangular plot in their backyard. Find the length of the diagonal of their garden.

2. Televisions are referred to by the diagonal of the screen. If a 40 inch television has a width of 32 inches, what is the height?

3. The diagonal of a square is $6\sqrt{2}$ units. What is the length of a side of the square?

4. A ramp is being built by a construction company. They need to make sure that the length of the ramp is one foot longer than the base. The other leg needs to be 5 feet high. Find the length of the ramp.

5. If one leg of a right triangle is $5\sqrt{3}$ centimeters and the hypotenuse is 2 more than the other leg, what is the length of the other leg?

Exponential Growth

Use $P(t) = P_0e^{kt}$ where P_0 is number at time 0, t is time (in years), k is growth rate, and $P(t)$ is amount at time t. Round answers to the nearest tenth.

1. Suppose that Mexico's growth rate is currently 2.4%. Their population is approximately 105 million people.

   (a) What will their population be in 10 years?

   (b) How long will it take their population to double?

2. The world population in 1900 was approximately 1.5 billion. If the population growth was 2%, what would the population be in 1950?

3. In 2000, the population of the world was approximately 6 billion. If the population growth rate of the world is approximately 1.3%,

   (a) What will the population be in 2015?

   (b) How long will it take to triple the population?

4. A rare coin was bought in 1900 for $0.25. In 2003 it was worth $250.

   (a) What is the exponential growth rate for how much the coin is worth?

   (b) Supposing that the growth rate (rounded to the nearest tenth) remains constant, what will the coin be worth in 2025?

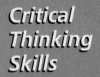

Compound Interest

Use $A = P(1 + r/n)^{nt}$ to help solve the following problems, where A = total amount, P = principal invested, r = rate of interest (expressed as a decimal), n = number of times per year interest is compounded, t = number of years invested. Round answers to the nearest tenth.

1. Determine how much money you will have if you invest $150 for 3 years at 8% compounded monthly.

2. After 6 years an investment is worth $6922.06. If the money was invested at 4.5% interest compounded semiannually (two times per year), find the original amount that was invested.

3. You are given two options to invest $750 that you have saved from work. You plan on leaving the money in the account for 5 years. The first option is to invest it in a Certificate of Deposit that yields 6% compounded annually. The second option is to invest it in a Money Market account at a rate of 5.5% compounded monthly. Which option is the better investment? By how much?

4. You invest $3000 in an account that earns 7.5% annual interest compounded quarterly (four times per year). How long will it take the account to double?

5. You put $1600 in an account at 8% interest compounded semi-annually. How long will it take the account to earn $800 in interest?

© RBP Books

Looking for a Pattern

Identify a pattern and use it to find the next three numbers.

1. 4, 2, 0, -2, …

2. 9, 3, 1, $\frac{1}{3}$, $\frac{1}{9}$, …

3. 0, 3, 8, 15, 24, …

4. 0, 2, -1, 1, -2, 0, …

5. 3, 6, 11, 18, 27, …

6. 2, 3, 5, 8, 13, 21, …

7. 4, 6, 8, 9, 10, 12, 14, 15, 16, …

8. 1, $\frac{2}{3}$, $\frac{4}{9}$, $\frac{8}{27}$, …

9. 1, 4, 9, 16, …

10. 5, 2, 10, 4, 20, 8, …

Answer Pages

Page 1

1. 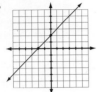 **2.**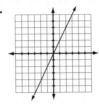

3. 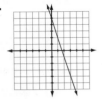 **4.**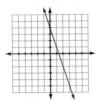

Page 2

1. (0,1) (-2,0) **2.** (0,-2) (5,0)

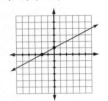 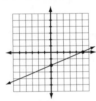

3. (3,0) (0,-5) **4.** (-1,0) (0,-3)

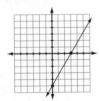 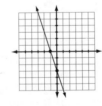

5. (0,-8) (4,0) **6.** (-2,0) (0,6)

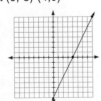 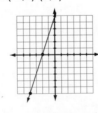

Page 3

1. $-\frac{1}{2}$ **2.** $\frac{1}{3}$ **3.** 1 **4.** 0

5. 1 **6.** $\frac{6}{5}$ **7.** -2 **8.** $\frac{7}{4}$

Page 4

1.   **2.**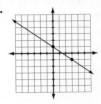

3. 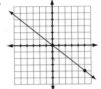 **4.**

5. 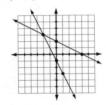 **6.**

Page 5

1. (-2,3) **2.** (-1,2)

3. (4,3) **4.** no solution

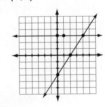 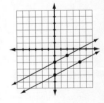

Page 6

1. (5,1) **2.** (1,4) **3.** (-4,-2) **4.** (2,-2)

Page 7

1. $(-4,\frac{1}{3})$ **2.** (3,-1) **3.** (3,2) **4.** (4,0)

© RBP Books

Answer Pages

Page 8

1. $4a^5 - 7a + 3$
2. $5x^6 - 4x^5 + 5x^3 - 6x^2 - 14$
3. $-19x^2 + 5x + 7$
4. $12x^6 + 13x^5 + 32x^4 - 12x^3 + 16x$
5. $-18x^2 + 18x - 21$
6. $7x^2 + 3x - 2$
7. $29x^2 + 4x + 14$
8. $14x^7 - 13x^6 + 18x^5 + 7x^4 - 5x^2 - 8x + 11$
9. $-8x^2 - 14x - 5$
10. $15x^7 + 12x^5 + 20x^4 + 6x^3 - 8x - 14$

Page 9

1. x^6 2. $\dfrac{x^4}{y^4}$ 3. a^8 4. $\dfrac{1}{w^5}$ 5. $16b^4$

6. $\dfrac{1}{b^2}$ 7. $9d^{10}$ 8. $\dfrac{x}{2}$ 9. m^{14} 10. k^2

Page 10

1. $-60x^2 - 36x$
2. $40x^5 - 48x^4 - 4x^3 + 32x^2$
3. $15x^2 + 12x$
4. $54x^5 - 90x^3$
5. $-9x^3 - 3x^2 + 5x$
6. $x^7 + \dfrac{3}{2}x^3 + 2$
7. $-3x^{10} - \dfrac{7}{2}x^7 + \dfrac{9}{2}$
8. $\dfrac{1}{2}x^9 - \dfrac{1}{2}x^6 - 3x^3$
9. $-2x^9 + 3x^8 - \dfrac{2}{3}x^2 + \dfrac{7}{3}$
10. $3x^3 - 4x^2 + 4x + 9 + \dfrac{34}{11x}$

Page 11

1. $16x^2 + 42x - 49$
2. $-40x^5 + 40x^4 - 28x^3 + 28x^2$
3. $-48x^3 - 28x^2 - 126x + 22$
4. $40x^6 - 88x^5 + 68x^4 - 24x^3 + 16x^2 - 16x + 8$
5. $-24x + 72$
6. $-44x^5 - 61x^4 + 28x^3$
7. $44x^3 + 49x^2 - 17x + 56$
8. $100x^4 - 70x^3 - 50x^2 - 165x - 90$

Page 12

1. $-3x^2 - 27x$ 2. $-x^2 - 4x$

3. $x^2 + 2x - 3 + \dfrac{3}{4x - 1}$

4. $-2x^2 - 18x$

5. $-3x^2 - 6x + \dfrac{5}{x - 3}$

Page 13

1. $3(a^2 + a - 2)$
2. $2y^3(y + 7)$
3. $4b(b^2 - 2b + 4)$
4. $6e(5e - 2f + ef^2)$
5. $4(d^3 - ad + a^2)$
6. $4w^3x(7 + 2w)$
7. $4r^6(3 + 2r - 8r^2 + 9r^3)$
8. $10ce(d + 2f - 3g)$

Page 14

1. $(x - 9)(x + 7)$ 2. $(x - 5)(x - 5)$
3. $(x + 1)(x + 1)$ 4. $(2x + 1)(x - 3)$
5. $(4x + 3)(2x - 3)$ 6. $(3x - 2)(x + 4)$
7. $(3x + 2)(4x + 5)$ 8. $(2x + 5)(3x + 4)$

Page 15

1. $x(x - 9)(x + 4)$ 2. $3(x - 12)(x + 4)$
3. $-4x(x - 8)(x - 8)$ 4. $3x(x - 8)(x + 6)$
5. $x(x + 8)(x - 11)$ 6. $-3x(x - 5)(x - 10)$
7. $6x^2(x - 10)(x + 1)$ 8. $2x^2(x - 11)(x - 12)$

Page 16

1. $(x - 11)(x + 11)$
2. $(2x - 9)(2x + 9)$
3. $(9y^2 - 8xy)(9y^2 + 8xy)$
4. $(a + 3)(a^2 - 3a + 9)$
5. $(bc^2 - 1)(b^2c^4 + bc^2 + 1)$
6. $(3z + 1)(9z^2 - 3z + 1)$
7. $(5c^2 - 2d^3)(25c^4 + 10c^2d^3 + 4d^6)$
8. $(4 - 5x)(16 + 20x + 25x^2)$
9. $(\dfrac{1}{6} - m)(\dfrac{1}{6} + m)$
10. $2y(y - 4)(y^2 + 4y + 16)$

Page 17

1. $\dfrac{14}{x^2y^2z^2}$ 2. $\dfrac{m^4}{n^3p}$

3. $\dfrac{3f^5}{14}$ 4. $\dfrac{1}{(w - 2)(w - 3)}$

5. $\dfrac{(f - 5)(f - 9)}{-7f^3(f - 1)}$ 6. $\dfrac{2(d^2 - 2)}{5d}$

73

Answer Pages

Page 18

1. $\dfrac{5x^4}{2y^4z^2}$

2. $16m^2np^2$

3. $\dfrac{16}{81y}$

4. $\dfrac{(x-9)(x+1)}{-3x^2(x-2)}$

5. $\dfrac{-7}{3(f+3)^2}$

6. $\dfrac{2}{(x^3-2)(x+2)}$

Page 19

1. $\dfrac{11a}{6}$

2. $\dfrac{29h}{32}$

3. $\dfrac{4h-6q}{qh}$

4. $\dfrac{2d-1}{8}$

5. $\dfrac{-3d^2+6d+2}{6d^2}$

6. $\dfrac{11d}{10}$

7. $\dfrac{7e+8}{10(f+1)}$

8. $\dfrac{-20c^2+5c-7}{12c(3c+2)}$

Page 20

1. $\dfrac{31}{4}$

2. 2

3. no solution

4. 5

5. $\dfrac{3}{2}$

6. $\dfrac{85}{12}$

Page 21

1. $2g^2d\sqrt{d}$

2. $\dfrac{9}{4}$

3. $7b^3ek^2\sqrt{be}$

4. 2

5. $-10fkd^2c^3\sqrt[3]{k^2d^2c^2}$

6. $\dfrac{-2k^3\sqrt[3]{25k^2}}{3}$

7. $-3m^3j^2\sqrt[4]{m^2j}$

8. $\dfrac{5e}{6}$

9. $\dfrac{-3f}{2}$

10. $(y-2)\sqrt[5]{8(y-2)}$

Page 22

1. $2\sqrt{3}$

2. 0

3. $\sqrt{3}+5\sqrt{11}$

4. $2\sqrt[3]{5}-\sqrt[3]{6}+3\sqrt[3]{20}$

5. $-12\sqrt[3]{3}$

6. $30+5\sqrt{3x}$

7. $\sqrt[4]{2y}+y\sqrt{y}$

8. $4x^2+(-2x^2-x)\sqrt{x}$

Page 23

1. $4c^3e\sqrt{2de}$

2. $7b\sqrt{2bc}$

3. $x^2y^7\sqrt[3]{xy}$

4. $x\sqrt[3]{75x^2y^2}$

5. $3(y+2)^{10}\sqrt{2}$

6. $8x^2+6x\sqrt{3}+3$

7. $7+7\sqrt{5y}$

8. 61

Page 24

1. $\dfrac{2\sqrt{5}}{5}$

2. $\sqrt{2}$

3. $\dfrac{\sqrt{3}}{2}$

4. $\dfrac{\sqrt[3]{45}}{3}$

5. $\dfrac{25+5\sqrt{11}}{14}$

6. $\dfrac{-12-3\sqrt{3}}{13}$

7. $7+4\sqrt{3}$

8. $\dfrac{x^2-x\sqrt{6}+x\sqrt{3}-3\sqrt{2}}{x^2-6}$

Page 25

1. 9

2. 5

3. $\dfrac{19}{2}$

4. -8

5. 78

6. -63

7. 5

8. 7

Page 26

1. i

2. -1

3. -1

4. 1

5. i

6. 1

7. 1

8. $2i$

9. i

10. 0

Page 27

1. $2\sqrt{15}-4i\sqrt{3}$

2. $8-i$

3. $88-7i\sqrt{2}$

4. 42

5. $3+i\sqrt{6}$

6. $-12+4i$

7. 25

8. $3\sqrt{2}+6i$

9. $43+6i$

10. $6-8i$

Page 28

1. $x^{2/3}$

2. $x^{1/5}y^{2/5}z^{3/5}$ or $(xy^2z^3)^{1/5}$

3. $\left(\dfrac{4b}{3a}\right)^{3/5}$

4. $6^{3/28}$

5. $2^{13/20}$

6. $x^{6/7}$

7. $g^{23/12}$

8. x^5y^6

9. $\dfrac{d^{7/18}}{c^{3/2}}$

10. $(xy)^{1/6}$ or $x^{1/6}y^{1/6}$

Answer Pages

Page 29
1. -7, 4   **2.** $-\frac{1}{2}$, 4   **3.** -1, $\frac{1}{3}$ **4.** 4, -4

5. -4, 8   **6.** 0, 6   **7.** -1, 1   **8.** 0, -2, 3

Page 30
1. 9, -9   **2.** -2, 2   **3.** $\frac{4}{3}$, $-\frac{4}{3}$ **4.** 3, -7

5. -7, 3   **6.** $2 \pm 2i$ **7.** -1, $-\frac{1}{3}$ **8.** $-\frac{1}{2} \pm i\sqrt{5}$

Page 31
1. $-6 \pm 4\sqrt{2}$ **2.** 9, -1

3. $2 \pm \sqrt{11}$ **4.** $\dfrac{9 \pm i\sqrt{19}}{2}$

5. $\frac{1}{2}$, $-\frac{3}{2}$ **6.** $2\sqrt{3}$

Page 32
1. 1, $\frac{1}{4}$ **2.** $3 \pm \sqrt{5}$

3. $\dfrac{-3 \pm i\sqrt{71}}{10}$ **4.** $\dfrac{-3 \pm i\sqrt{23}}{2}$

5. 8, $\frac{6}{5}$ **6.** $\dfrac{9 \pm \sqrt{33}}{8}$

Page 33
1.

2.

3.

4.

Page 34
1. 6, -3   **2.** $\pm4\sqrt{2} \approx \pm5.66$

3. 0, 6   **4.** $\dfrac{8 \pm \sqrt{2}}{3} \approx 3.14, 2.20$

5. $\dfrac{-1 \pm \sqrt{5}}{2} \approx -1.62, .62$

6. $\dfrac{15 \pm \sqrt{465}}{6} \approx 6.09, -1.09$

Page 35
1. (-1,2)   **2.** (1,1)

3. $(\frac{1}{2}, -6\frac{1}{4})$ **4.** (-4,0)

5. (-1,3)   **6.** $(\frac{6}{5}, -27\frac{1}{5})$

Page 36
1.

2.
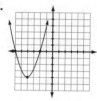

3.
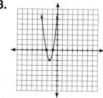

4.
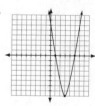

Page 37
1. a) 222   b) 54   c) 39   d) 19

2. a) -1   b) 64   c) -125   d) $8m^3$

3. a) 7   b) 6   c) 16   d) $x^2 + 2$

Page 38
1. D: all reals, R: $y \geq -3$

2. D: all reals, R: $y \geq -3$

3. D: $x \neq 0$, R: $y \neq 0$

4. D: all reals, R: all reals

5. D: all reals, R: all reals

6. D: all reals, R: $y \leq 0$

Page 39
1. $3x^2 - 8$ **2.** $x^2 + 6x + 8$

3. $3x - 2$ **4.** $9x^2 - 30x + 24$

5. $3x + 4$ **6.** $3x^2 + 1$

Answer Pages

Page 40

1. $5x^3 - x^2 - 10x + 2$ **2.** $x^2 + 3x - 2$
3. $3x^3 - 6x$ **4.** $-x^2 + 5x + 1$
5. 98 **6.** -63

Page 41

1. Function and 1-1
2. Function, not 1-1
3. Function and 1-1
4. Neither function nor 1-1

Page 42

1. $f^{-1}(x) = \frac{1}{4}x + 2$ **2.** $f^{-1}(x) = \frac{1}{3}x - 2$

3. $f^{-1}(x) = 2x + 2$ **4.** $f^{-1}(x) = \frac{3}{2}x - 6$

5. $f^{-1}(x) = \dfrac{4}{5(x+3)}$ **6.** $f^{-1}(x) = \sqrt[3]{x}$

Page 43

1. 3 **2.** $\frac{3}{2}$ **3.** -2 **4.** 1
5. $-\frac{1}{2}$ **6.** -1 **7.** -6 **8.** $\frac{4}{3}$

Page 44

1. $\log_3 81 = 4$ **2.** $\log_{10} 0.1 = -1$
3. $\log_8 \frac{1}{2} = -\frac{1}{3}$ **4.** $\log_{10} 10000 = 4$
5. $\log_{15} 225\sqrt{15} = \frac{5}{2}$ **6.** $2^3 = 8$
7. $5^3 = 125$ **8.** $3^{-3} = \frac{1}{27}$
9. $3.2^1 = 3.2$ **10.** $(\frac{2}{3})^{-3} = \frac{27}{8}$

Page 45

1. 5 **2.** 1000 **3.** 9 **4.** -1
5. -2 **6.** -2 **7.** 1 **8.** -5

Page 46

1. 0.568 **2.** 2.508 **3.** -1.301 **4.** 1.079
5. 2.283 **6.** 1.504 **7.** 4.127 **8.** 6.461
9. 13.122 **10.** 4.585

Page 47

1. 9183.326 **2.** 1.056
3. 0.455 **4.** 0.105
5. 3.684 **6.** 5585.895
7. 1.087 **8.** 0.006

Page 48

1. 0.944 **2.** 2 **3.** 2.814 **4.** -1.135
5. 1 **6.** 0.778 **7.** -5.672 **8.** 0.803
9. 2.096 **10.** 5.904

Page 49

1. 1.34 **2.** 9.83 **3.** 1.93 **4.** 0.64
5. -0.27 **6.** 12.02

Page 50

1. $\log_4 3 + \log_4 y$ **2.** $\log_a b - \log_a c$

3. $\frac{1}{2}\log_4 5$ **4.** $\log_5 2 + 3\log_5 x$

5. $2y(\log_b x - \log_b 5)$ **6.** $\log_4(xyz)$

7. $\log_2 m^5 n$ **8.** $\log_3(\frac{\sqrt{x}}{y})$

9. $\log_3(\frac{a}{b^{1/4}})$ **10.** $\log_4(\frac{xy}{z})$

Page 51

1. $\sqrt{3}$ **2.** 8 **3.** 1 **4.** $\sqrt{6}$
5. 7, -7 **6.** $\frac{4}{3}$

Page 52

1. 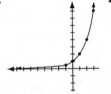 **2.**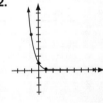

3. **4.**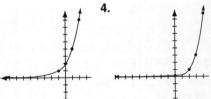

Answer Pages

Page 53

1. 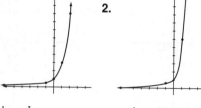 **2.**

3. **4.**

The graph gets steeper.
The graph is flipped around the y-axis.

Page 54

1.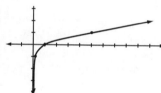

2.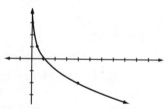

3.

4.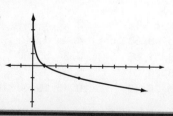

Page 55

1.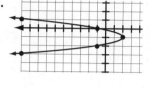

x	y
-1	0
-1	-2
10	1
10	-3

vertex
(2, -1)

2.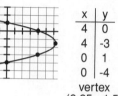

x	y
4	0
4	-3
0	1
0	-4

vertex
(6.25, -1.5)

Page 56

1. 4   **2.** 10   **3.** $6\sqrt{5}$ **4.** $7\sqrt{5}$

5. $\sqrt{2}$ **6.** $2\sqrt{10}$ **7.** $5\sqrt{2}$ **8.** $2\sqrt{5}$

Page 57

1. (2,-3), 3   **2.** (4,6), $\sqrt{55}$

3. (5,4), 4   **4.** $(-\frac{7}{2},4)$, $\frac{\sqrt{93}}{2}$

5. (0,1), 6   **6.** (-5,0), $3\sqrt{2}$

Page 58

1.   **2.**

3.   **4.**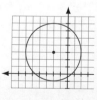

Page 59

1.   **2.**

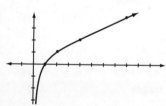

Answer Pages

Page 61

1.

2.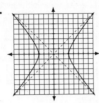

3.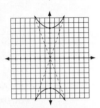

4.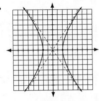

5.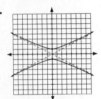

6.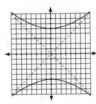

Page 62

1. Parabola

2. Ellipse

3. Parabola

4. Circle

5. Ellipse

6. Parabola

7. Hyperbola

8. Circle

9. Hyperbola

10. Hyperbola

11. Ellipse

12. Hyperbola

Page 63

1. f **2.** d **3.** e **4.** b

5. c **6.** a

Page 64

1. (4,0) (-4,0) **2.** (0,5) (-5,0)

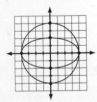 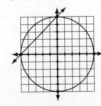

3. no solution **4.** (4,4) (1,-2)

 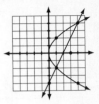

Page 65

1. 34 dimes, 66 nickels

2. 18 pounds of peanuts

3. $7 \frac{1}{2}$ cups

4. $564 at 14%, $1536 at 18%

5. $42 in savings, $82 in mutual fund

Page 66

1. $6 \frac{1}{2}$ hours **2.** $93 \frac{1}{3}$ miles

3. 180 mph **4.** $4 \frac{1}{2}$ hours

5. $13 \frac{1}{5}$ mph

Page 67

1. 42.35 mph **2.** 49.5 mph

3. 48 mph **4.** 6 hours

5. 10 hours 40 minutes

Page 68

1. 50 feet **2.** 24 inches

3. 6 units **4.** 13 feet

5. 17.75 centimeters

Page 69

1. (a) 133.5 million (b) 28.9 years

2. 4.1 billion

3. (a) 7.3 billion (b) 84.5 years

4. (a) 6.7% (b) $1091.67

Page 70

1. $190.54 **2.** $5300

3. CD by $16.89 **4.** 9.3 years

5. 5.2 years

Page 71

1. -4, -6, -8 **2.** $\frac{1}{27}, \frac{1}{81}, \frac{1}{243}$

3. 35, 48, 63 **4.** -3, -1, -4

5. 38, 51, 66 **6.** 34, 55, 89

7. 18, 20, 21 **8.** $\frac{16}{81}, \frac{32}{243}, \frac{64}{729}$

9. 25, 36, 49 **10.** 40, 16, 80